5 W'S TO SUCCESS

5 W's to Success

Gibson Groft

Revival Fitness

Contents

Introduction

In the intricate journey of life, where each day presents new challenges and opportunities, finding true success often feels elusive. However, anchored in the unwavering love of God, I have found that we can navigate any circumstance and thrive in every aspect of our lives. Welcome to *5 W's to Success*, the second book in the *God's Love Unveiled* series. My name is Gibson Groft, and I invite you to explore with me the principles that have guided my journey from chaos to a life of purpose and fulfillment. In my first book, I shared my story of discovering the profound love and purpose that God has for each one of us. We explored the transformative power of God's love, delving into themes of forgiveness, redemption, resilience, and the importance of community. Through my personal experiences and reflections, we uncovered the truth that God's love is a constant source of solace and strength, guiding us through life's storms and leading us to a life filled with purpose and joy. As a 16-year-old junior at CTEC High School, my journey has been marked by both trials and triumphs. Growing up amidst the dichotomy of a Christ-centered home with my mom and an absence of the Holy Spirit at my dad's house, I experienced the tumultuous waves of confusion and conflict. My parents' divorce left deep scars, and I grappled with personal demons and internalized anger. Yet, amidst this turmoil, I found Christ and began a transformative journey that reshaped my life. At 14, I re-dedicated my life to Christ, and since then, God has been revealing His love and purpose for me, guiding me to a place of mental peace and spiritual growth. In "5 W's to Success," I build upon the foundation laid in "God's Love Unveiled" by diving deeper into the principles that lead to true success. These principles, rooted in wisdom, work, witness, waiting, and winning, are not mere steps but a holistic approach to living a life that glorifies God and fulfills His purpose for us. Moreover, my passion for fitness and my aspiration of becoming a fitness trainer and owning my gym are integral parts of my journey. Fitness, to me, is not just about physical strength but about honoring God with our bodies, living a healthy lifestyle that reflects His care and love for us. As you read through this book, I hope to inspire you to seek God's wisdom, work diligently with a sense of purpose, be a witness to His love, wait patiently on His timing, and celebrate your victories with gratitude. By incorporating these principles into every area of your life, including your physical well-being, you can achieve true success and live a life that honors God in every way.

The 5 W's are as follows:

Wisdom:

Every endeavor begins with heartfelt worship and prayer, acknowledging that our strength and guidance come from

God. By dedicating time to connect with Him, we lay a solid foundation for all our actions, ensuring that our goals align with His purpose. Wisdom is not just about making the right decisions but about seeking God's guidance in everything we do. In my own life, I have found that starting my day with prayer and worship sets the tone for everything that follows. It helps me align my intentions with God's will and gives me the clarity and strength to face whatever challenges come my way. Proverbs 3:5-6 says, "Trust in the Lord with all your heart and lean not on your own understanding; in all your ways submit to him, and he will make your paths straight." This verse has been a guiding light for me, reminding me that true wisdom comes from trusting God and seeking His guidance in all aspects of life. When I was younger, I often relied on my own understanding, making decisions based on what seemed logical or convenient at the time. This approach led to confusion and mistakes, reinforcing the importance of seeking God's wisdom. By dedicating time to worship and prayer, I have learned to trust in God's plan, knowing that His wisdom far surpasses my own. This principle of wisdom is the foundation for success in every area of life, guiding us to make choices that align with God's purpose and lead us toward a fulfilling and meaningful existence.

Work:

Success requires diligent and wholehearted effort. Colossians 3:23 reminds us to work with all our heart as if working for the Lord. Through consistent and dedicated work, we achieve our goals and demonstrate our faith in action, glorifying God. In my journey, I have learned that hard work is essential to achieving success. It's not just about putting in the hours but about working with a sense of purpose and dedication, knowing that our efforts are for God's glory. When I was younger, I struggled with motivation and often procrastinated, leading to stress and subpar results. However, as I grew in my faith, I realized that working diligently is a form of worship, an opportunity to honor God with the talents and abilities He has given us. Whether it's in my studies, my writing, or my involvement in student leadership, I strive to work with excellence, giving my best in everything I do. This principle of work is not just about achieving personal success but about using our efforts to serve others and make a positive impact in the world. By working diligently and wholeheartedly, we reflect God's character and inspire those around us to do the same. In the parable of the talents (Matthew 25:14-30), Jesus teaches us the importance of using our gifts wisely and working diligently to multiply what we have been given. This parable has been a powerful reminder for me to be a good steward of the opportunities and talents God has entrusted to me, working with all my heart as if for the Lord.

Witness:

Our lives are a testimony to our faith. By serving others and sharing our journey, we create a ripple effect of kindness and encouragement. Matthew 5:16 encourages us to let our light shine, inspiring others and building a supportive community. Being a witness is about more than just speaking about our faith; it's about living it out in our daily actions and interactions. In my own life, I have seen the impact that a positive witness can have on those around me. By showing kindness, compassion, and integrity, I have been able to inspire and encourage others, creating a supportive community of believers. When I was struggling with my faith, it was the witness of others that helped me see the love and grace of God. Their actions spoke louder than words, showing me the power of living a Christ-centered life. Now, I strive to be that same light for others, serving those around me and sharing my journey of faith. This principle of witness is about being intentional in our actions, knowing that we are representing Christ to the world. In my school, in my community, and in my writing, I aim to let my light shine, demonstrating the love and grace of God through my actions. By doing so, I hope to inspire others to seek a relationship with Christ and to create a ripple effect of kindness and encouragement that extends far beyond my own reach.

Wait:

Patience and perseverance are crucial. Isaiah 40:31 reassures us that those who wait on the Lord will renew their strength. Waiting involves active trust and preparation, embracing challenges as opportunities for growth, knowing that God's plan unfolds in His perfect timing. In my journey, I have learned that waiting is not about inactivity but about trusting in God's timing and being patient in the process. When I was younger, I often struggled with impatience, wanting immediate results and quick fixes. However, through my experiences, I have come to understand the value of waiting on the Lord. It is during these times of waiting that God often does His deepest work in our hearts, refining our character and preparing us for the next season of life. One of the most challenging periods of waiting for me was during my parents' divorce. It was a time of uncertainty and pain, but through it, I learned to trust in God's plan and to rely on His strength. Isaiah 40:31 became a lifeline for me, reminding me that those who wait on the Lord will renew their strength. This principle of waiting has taught me to embrace challenges as opportunities for growth and to trust that God's timing is perfect. By waiting on the Lord, we are renewed and strengthened, ready to face whatever lies ahead with faith and confidence.

Win:

Embracing a winning mindset means celebrating progress and achievements with gratitude. 1 Corinthians 9:24 reminds us to run in such a way as to get the prize. By maintaining a positive attitude and recognizing our hard work, we stay humble and committed to continuous growth. In my journey, I have learned the importance of celebrating victories, no matter how small. It's easy to get caught up in the pursuit of the next goal and to overlook the progress we have made. However, taking time to celebrate our achievements helps us to stay motivated and to recognize the blessings in our lives. When I was younger, I often struggled with self-doubt and negative thinking, which made it difficult to see my own progress. However, as I grew in my faith, I began to embrace a winning mindset, celebrating each victory with gratitude and humility. This principle of winning is not just about achieving success but about maintaining a positive attitude and a heart full of gratitude. By doing so, we stay humble and committed to continuous growth, knowing that every achievement is a gift from God. 1 Corinthians 9:24 reminds us to run in such a way as to get the prize, encouraging us to stay focused and to give our best in everything we do. In my own life, I strive to maintain this winning mindset, celebrating each step forward and recognizing the hard work that has brought me success.

One

Wisdom

In the quest for true success, wisdom stands as the foundational pillar that aligns our lives with God's purpose, guiding our decisions and actions with divine insight. Wisdom, as the Bible teaches, begins with the fear of the Lord, a deep reverence and acknowledgment of His sovereignty and love. For me, wisdom is not just about making the right decisions but about seeking God's guidance in everything I do. In my own life, I have found that starting each day with heartfelt worship and prayer sets the tone for everything that follows. By dedicating time to connect with God, I align my intentions with His will, finding clarity and strength to face whatever challenges come my way. Proverbs 3:5-6 has been a guiding light for me, saying, "Trust in the Lord with all your heart and lean not on your own understanding; in all your ways submit to him, and he will make your paths straight." This verse reminds me that true wisdom comes from trusting God and seeking His guidance in all aspects of life. When I was younger, I often relied on my own understanding, making decisions based on what seemed logical or convenient at the time. This approach led to confusion and mistakes, reinforcing the importance of seeking God's wisdom. By dedicating time to worship and prayer, I have learned to trust in God's plan, knowing that His wisdom far surpasses my own. This principle of wisdom is the foundation for success in every area of life, guiding us to make choices that align with God's purpose and lead us toward a fulfilling and meaningful existence. Additionally, wisdom manifests in how we treat our bodies, recognizing that maintaining physical health is a form of honoring God. My passion for fitness and my dream of becoming a fitness trainer and owning my gym are deeply intertwined with my spiritual journey. In 1 Corinthians 6:19-20, Paul reminds us that our bodies are temples of the Holy Spirit, and we are to honor God with them. This wisdom has driven me to adopt a lifestyle that emphasizes physical health, not just for personal gain but as an act of worship and stewardship of the body God has given me. Through my experiences, I have seen how a disciplined approach to fitness and health can lead to greater mental clarity, emotional stability, and spiritual growth. It's a holistic approach where physical well-being supports and enhances our spiritual journey. Wisdom also involves learning from others, seeking counsel, and being open to correction. Proverbs 12:15 says, "The way of fools seems right to them, but the wise listen to advice." Throughout my journey, I have been blessed with mentors and a supportive community who have guided me, offering wisdom and encouragement. Their insights have helped me navigate the complexities of life, reinforcing the importance of community in our pursuit of wisdom. Ultimately, wisdom is about living in a way that reflects God's love and purpose in every aspect of our lives. It requires humility, a willingness to seek God's guidance, and a commitment to living in accordance with His will. By embracing wisdom, we lay a solid foundation for all our actions, ensuring that our goals align with God's purpose and that we move forward with divine support. As you reflect on this principle, I encourage you to seek God's wisdom daily, through prayer, worship, and the study of His Word. Allow His guidance to shape your decisions, influence your actions, and lead you toward a life of true success and fulfillment, honoring Him in all that you do.

Wisdom, often depicted as the wise sage or the all-knowing mentor, is more than just a concept—it's a way of life. It's the art of discerning right from wrong, good from bad, and making decisions that align with God's will. For me, wisdom isn't merely about accumulating knowledge or spouting off wise-sounding phrases; it's about embodying principles that lead to a life of purpose and fulfillment. It's about recognizing the limitations of our own understanding and seeking divine guidance in every aspect of life. Growing up in a world inundated with information, where opinions masquerade as facts and noise drowns out wisdom, the pursuit of true wisdom has become increasingly challenging. It requires a deliberate effort to sift through the clutter, to discern truth from falsehood, and to align our hearts with God's truth. It's a journey marked by humility, as we acknowledge that true wisdom comes not from our own intellect but from a deep and abiding relationship with the Creator of the universe. Proverbs, often referred to as the book of wisdom, offers timeless insights into the nature of wisdom and its practical implications for daily living. Proverbs 2:6 tells us that "For the Lord gives wisdom; from his mouth come knowledge and understanding." This verse reminds us that true wisdom originates from God Himself, and it is through His word that we gain understanding and insight into the mysteries of life. But wisdom is more than just theoretical knowledge; it's about how we apply that knowledge in our lives. It's about making decisions that honor God and benefit ourselves and others. It's about seeking counsel from those who have walked the path before us and being open to correction when we stray from the path of wisdom. It's about recognizing that wisdom often requires us to take the road less traveled, to make choices that may not always be popular but are aligned with God's truth. In my own journey, I've seen the transformative power of wisdom at work. From navigating the complexities of relationships to making career decisions, wisdom has been my guiding light, leading me through the darkest of times and illuminating the path ahead. It's through wisdom that I've learned to recognize the difference between fleeting happiness and lasting joy, between temporary success and true fulfillment. Moreover, wisdom extends beyond individual choices to encompass broader societal issues. In a world plagued by division and discord, wisdom calls us to seek understanding, to bridge the gap between opposing viewpoints, and to work towards reconciliation and unity. It's through wisdom that we navigate the complexities of a rapidly changing world, discerning the signs of the times and responding with grace and wisdom. In conclusion, wisdom is not just a virtue to be admired from afar but a principle to be embraced and embodied in our daily lives. It's about seeking God's guidance in every decision, trusting in His wisdom above our own, and allowing His truth to shape our thoughts, words, and actions. As we embark on the journey towards true success, may we walk in the footsteps of the wise, seeking wisdom above all else and allowing it to guide us on the path to fulfillment and purpose.

Two

Work

Hard work is the cornerstone of success. It's the relentless pursuit of our dreams, the unwavering dedication to our goals, and the refusal to settle for mediocrity that propels us forward on the path to greatness. But beyond mere effort, true success demands a burning passion, a deep-seated desire to see our dreams become a reality. This journey of hard work is not just about putting in the hours or going through the motions; it's about pouring every ounce of energy and enthusiasm into the pursuit of our goals, knowing that the journey will be arduous but ultimately rewarding. Throughout my journey, I've encountered countless obstacles and setbacks, moments when it would have been easier to throw in the towel and admit defeat. Yet, it's in those moments of adversity that the true test of character emerges. It's when we're faced with unforeseen circumstances, when our carefully laid plans are disrupted, that we have the opportunity to grow and learn. Each setback becomes a lesson in resilience, teaching us to adapt, to persevere, and to emerge stronger than before. The path to success is not without its challenges. It's a journey fraught with uncertainty, where success is never guaranteed and failure lurks around every corner. Yet, it's precisely in the face of adversity that our faith is tested and our resolve strengthened. It's in those moments of doubt and uncertainty that we're called to trust in God's plan, to surrender our fears and insecurities, and to press on with unwavering determination. But even amidst the challenges and uncertainties, hard work remains a constant companion—a guiding light that illuminates the path ahead. Work is not just about achieving our own personal goals; it's about serving a higher purpose and fulfilling God's calling on our lives. Colossians 3:23 reminds us that "whatever you do, work at it with all your heart, as working for the Lord, not for human masters." This verse serves as a powerful reminder that our work is ultimately an act of worship—a way to honor God and glorify His name. In my own journey towards success, I've learned that hard work alone is not enough. It must be accompanied by wisdom, discernment, and a willingness to follow God's guidance every step of the way. It's about seeking His will in every decision, trusting in His timing, and surrendering our desires to His perfect plan. It's a delicate balance between striving for excellence and surrendering to divine providence—a balance that can only be achieved through prayer, humility, and an unwavering faith in God's promises. As we embark on this journey, may we be reminded that true success is not measured by the accolades we receive or the wealth we amass, but by the lives we touch, the impact we make, and the legacy we leave behind. And may we always remember that with God by our side, no dream is too big, no obstacle too insurmountable, and no effort too small to make a difference. So let us roll up our sleeves, dig deep, and embark on this journey of hard work and faith, knowing that with God's grace, all things are possible.

Hard work is not just a concept; it's a commitment to excellence, a dedication to constant improvement, and a refusal to settle for anything less than our best. It's about setting lofty goals and then rolling up our sleeves and doing whatever it takes to achieve them. It's about embracing challenges as opportunities for growth, viewing setbacks as stepping stones to success, and persevering in the face of adversity. But beyond the physical effort, hard work also requires mental fortitude and emotional resilience. It's about staying focused and disciplined even when the going gets tough, maintaining a positive attitude and unwavering belief in ourselves and our abilities. It's about pushing through fatigue, doubt, and fear, and staying committed to our goals no matter what obstacles may arise. In my own journey, I've learned firsthand the transformative power of hard work. From a young age, I was taught the value of diligence and perseverance by my parents, who instilled in me a strong work ethic and a belief in the importance of giving my all to whatever I set my mind to. Whether it was academics, athletics, or personal pursuits, I was taught to approach every task with determination and enthusiasm, knowing that success would only come through hard work and dedication. As I grew older, I began to see the fruits of my labor firsthand. I discovered that hard work wasn't just about achieving external success or reaching specific milestones; it was about the personal growth and fulfillment that came from pushing myself beyond my limits and striving for excellence in everything I did. I learned that success wasn't just measured by the end result but by the effort and commitment that went into achieving it. But hard work is not just about personal achievement; it's also about serving others and making a positive impact on the world around us. Whether it's through our professional endeavors, our relationships, or our contributions to our community, hard work enables us to make a difference in the lives of others and leave a lasting legacy that extends far beyond our own individual accomplishments. Moreover, hard work is not a solitary endeavor; it's a collaborative effort that requires the support and encouragement of others. Whether it's family, friends, mentors, or colleagues, we all need a support system to lean on when times get tough, to offer guidance and wisdom when we falter, and to celebrate with us when we succeed. It's through the collective efforts of a community that we're able to achieve our greatest accomplishments and overcome our greatest challenges. In conclusion, hard work is the bedrock upon which success is built. It's the driving force that propels us forward, the fuel that sustains us through the long and arduous journey, and the key to unlocking our full potential. But hard work is not just about physical effort; it's also about mental toughness, emotional resilience, and unwavering commitment to our goals. It's about pushing ourselves beyond our comfort zones, embracing challenges as opportunities for growth, and staying true to our values and beliefs no matter what obstacles may come our way. So let us embrace the spirit of hard work wholeheartedly, knowing that with dedication, determination, and faith in ourselves and in God's plan, there is no limit to what we can achieve.

In a world where mediocrity often masquerades as excellence, truly giving our best sets us apart from the crowd. It's easy to coast through life, to settle for average, to make excuses for why we can't achieve our dreams. But greatness demands more—it demands our full commitment, our unwavering dedication, and our relentless pursuit of excellence. Most people never truly give their best because they're afraid of failure, afraid of the hard work and sacrifice required to succeed. They're content to stay within their comfort zones, to avoid taking risks, and to settle for less than they're capable of achieving. But the truth is that failure is not the result of giving our best; it's the result of holding back, of playing it safe, of settling for less than we're capable of. When we truly give 100 percent, when we pour every ounce of our energy and passion into the pursuit of our goals, failure is not an option. It's not about whether we succeed or fail; it's about knowing that we've given it everything we've got, that we've left no stone unturned in our quest for greatness. When we commit fully to our goals, when we refuse to let fear or doubt hold us back, we unleash our full potential and become unstoppable forces for change. But giving our best is not always easy. It requires discipline, perseverance, and an unwavering belief in ourselves and our abilities. It means pushing through fatigue, doubt, and fear, and staying focused on our goals even when the going gets tough. It means making sacrifices, putting in the extra hours, and doing whatever it takes to succeed. Yet, despite the challenges, giving our best is also incredibly rewarding. There's a deep sense of satisfaction that comes from knowing that we've given our all, that we've left nothing on the table, and that we've achieved something truly meaningful. And even if we don't always achieve the outcome we desire, we can take pride in the fact that we've given it our best shot and that we've grown stronger and more resilient in the process. In a world full of weak people, those who are truly willing to give their best stand head and shoulders above the rest. They are the ones who achieve greatness, who leave a lasting impact on the world, and who inspire others to follow in their footsteps. They are the ones who refuse to settle for mediocrity, who push the boundaries of what's possible, and who never stop striving for excellence. So let us not be content with mediocrity; let us strive for excellence in everything we do. Let us embrace the challenge of giving our best, knowing that with God's help and our unwavering commitment, there is no limit to what we can achieve. And let us inspire others to do the same, to rise above their fears and doubts, and to unleash their full potential on the world. For when we give our best, we not only transform our own lives but also the lives of those around us, leaving a legacy of excellence that will endure for generations to come.

Three

Witness

Being a witness to our faith is more than just a passive declaration of our beliefs; it's a call to action, a commitment to live out our values in tangible ways that make a positive impact on the world around us. Matthew 5:16 serves as a powerful reminder of our responsibility to let our light shine before others, not for our own glory, but so that they may see our good deeds and glorify our Father in heaven. For me, being a witness to my faith means embodying the principles of love, compassion, and service in everything I do. It's about looking beyond my own needs and desires and seeking opportunities to help those in need, to uplift the downtrodden, and to bring hope to the hopeless. Whether it's through volunteering at a local soup kitchen, participating in a community service project, or simply lending a listening ear to a friend in need, being a witness to my faith is about being a beacon of light in a world that often feels dark and hopeless.

But being a witness to our faith is not just about our actions; it's also about the way we live our lives and the example we set for others. It's about treating every person we encounter with kindness and respect, regardless of their background or beliefs. It's about being honest and transparent in our dealings with others, and striving to live with integrity and authenticity in all aspects of our lives. Moreover, being a witness to our faith is about sharing our journey with others—both the triumphs and the struggles. It's about being vulnerable and open about our own experiences, and using them to inspire and encourage others who may be facing similar challenges. It's about creating a safe space where people feel comfortable sharing their own stories and finding support and encouragement from others who have walked a similar path. One of the most powerful ways we can be a witness to our faith is through the power of our words. Whether it's through sharing our testimony with a friend, writing a blog post about our faith journey, or simply speaking words of encouragement to someone who is struggling, our words have the power to uplift, inspire, and bring hope to those around us. As the apostle Paul wrote in Ephesians 4:29, "Do not let any unwholesome talk come out of your mouths, but only what is helpful for building others up according to their needs, that it may benefit those who listen." But being a witness to our faith is not always easy. It requires courage, vulnerability, and a willingness to step out of our comfort zones. It means being willing to speak out against injustice, to stand up for what is right, and to be a voice for the voiceless. It means being willing to confront our own biases and prejudices, and to actively work towards building a more inclusive and equitable society.

The synergy between the work chapter and being a witness to our faith is paramount. While the work chapter emphasizes the importance of putting in the effort and dedication to achieve our goals, being a witness requires an additional layer of commitment and perseverance. It's not easy to live out our faith in a world that often opposes or misunderstands our beliefs. There will be obstacles—internal and external—that we must navigate with relentless determination. The challenges we face as witnesses may test our resolve and push us to our limits, but it's in these moments that the principles outlined in the work chapter come into play. We must work diligently to overcome these obstacles, whether they be doubts, fears, or opposition from others. Doubts can arise within us, questioning our abilities or the validity of our faith. We may wonder if we're truly making a difference or if our efforts are in vain. In these moments, it's essential to remind ourselves of the importance of our witness and the impact it can have on others. We must lean into our faith, trusting in God's plan and His ability to use even our smallest actions for His glory. External obstacles may also present themselves, ranging from societal pressures to outright persecution. In a world that often values success, wealth, and power above all else, living out our faith can be seen as counter-cultural and even threatening to some. We may face ridicule or discrimination for our beliefs, or we may encounter resistance from those who oppose the message of love and acceptance that lies at the heart of our faith. Yet, it's precisely in the face of such opposition that our witness shines brightest. Like a beacon of light in the darkness, our unwavering commitment to our faith stands as a testament to the transformative power of God's love. But overcoming these obstacles requires more than just sheer willpower; it requires a deep-rooted commitment to our values and beliefs. It requires us to align our actions with our convictions, even when doing so is difficult or uncomfortable. It means being willing to stand up for what is right, even when it's easier to remain silent. It means being a voice for the voiceless, a champion for the marginalized, and a beacon of hope for those who have lost their way. The work chapter provides us with a framework for navigating these challenges. It reminds us of the importance of perseverance, of staying focused on our goals even when the journey is difficult. It encourages us to lean into our faith, to trust in God's plan, and to rely on His strength to carry us through the darkest of times. And it reminds us that true success is not measured by the accolades we receive or the obstacles we overcome, but by the lives we touch and the hearts we inspire along the way. Moreover, the work chapter teaches us the importance of community in our journey as witnesses. We cannot do it alone; we need the support and encouragement of others to sustain us through the trials and tribulations of life. Surrounding ourselves with like-minded individuals who share our values and beliefs can provide us with the strength and courage we need to persevere in the face of adversity. Together, we can lift each other up, offering words of encouragement, a listening ear, or a helping hand when needed. And together, we can amplify our witness, spreading the message of God's love and grace to every corner of the earth. In conclusion, the work chapter and being a witness to our faith are intrinsically linked. They both require dedication, perseverance, and a willingness to overcome obstacles in pursuit of our goals. By combining the principles outlined in the work chapter with our commitment to being a witness, we can navigate the challenges of life with grace and resilience, knowing that with God by our side, all things are possible. So let us embrace the call to be witnesses to our faith, knowing that our efforts are not in vain and that our light shines brightest in the darkest of times.

Four

Wait

In a world that values instant gratification and immediate results, the concept of waiting can seem counterintuitive. We're bombarded with messages that tell us success should be instantaneous, that we should always be striving for more, faster, better. But the truth is that some of life's greatest blessings come to those who are willing to wait patiently and trust in God's perfect timing. Isaiah 40:31 offers a powerful reminder of the strength that comes from waiting on the Lord. It assures us that those who wait on Him will renew their strength, soar on wings like eagles, run and not grow weary, walk and not faint. This verse is a testament to the transformative power of patience and perseverance, and the profound impact it can have on our lives. But waiting is not synonymous with inactivity; it's about actively trusting and preparing during the process. It's about embracing challenges as opportunities to grow and refine our character, knowing that God's plan unfolds in His timing. Waiting requires us to relinquish control and surrender our desires to God's will, trusting that He knows what's best for us and that He will fulfill His promises in His own time and in His own way. One of the greatest challenges of waiting is learning to let go of our own timelines and expectations. We live in a society that values efficiency and productivity, often measuring our worth by our accomplishments and achievements. But God's timing is not bound by human constraints; His ways are higher than our ways, and His thoughts are higher than our thoughts. He sees the bigger picture, the broader scope of our lives, and He knows what we need before we even ask. Yet, waiting can be excruciatingly difficult, especially when we're faced with uncertainty or adversity. We may find ourselves grappling with doubt, wondering if God has forgotten about us or if our prayers are falling on deaf ears. But it's precisely in these moments of doubt and despair that our faith is tested and strengthened. It's when we cling to God's promises and hold fast to His word that we find the strength to persevere. Moreover, waiting is not a passive process; it's an active engagement with God and His plan for our lives. It's about seeking His will in every decision, listening for His voice in the midst of the chaos, and following His lead even when it doesn't make sense. It's about surrendering our desires and ambitions to Him, trusting that He knows what's best for us and that He will guide us along the right path. But waiting also requires us to cultivate a spirit of patience and contentment in the midst of uncertainty. It's about learning to be present in the moment, to appreciate the blessings that surround us, and to find joy in the journey, regardless of the destination. It's about recognizing that God's timing is perfect, even when it doesn't align with our own, and trusting that He has a purpose and a plan for our lives.

The concept of waiting is intricately connected to both the principles of work and witness in the journey of faith. While waiting may seem like a passive state of being, it is, in fact, a dynamic process that involves active engagement with God's plan for our lives. Waiting is not about idly sitting by and hoping for things to happen; it's about actively trusting and preparing during the process, all while continuing to work diligently and serve faithfully in accordance with God's will. Firstly, waiting and work go hand in hand in the journey of faith. Waiting does not mean inactivity; it means actively trusting and preparing during the process. As we wait for God's blessings and guidance, we are called to continue working diligently towards our goals, using our time, talents, and resources to glorify God and serve others. This principle is beautifully illustrated in the parable of the talents (Matthew 25:14-30), where the servants who faithfully put their talents to work were rewarded by their master. Similarly, as we wait for God's blessings on our endeavors, we are called to steward our gifts well and use them to advance His kingdom here on earth. Moreover, waiting provides us with an opportunity to grow and develop into the person God wants us to be. It's during the waiting season that God often refines and molds us, shaping our character and preparing us for the tasks ahead. As we work diligently and serve faithfully while waiting for God's blessings, we are transformed from the inside out, becoming more like Christ in our thoughts, words, and actions. This process of sanctification is essential for our spiritual growth and maturity, enabling us to fulfill God's purposes for our lives and impact the world around us in meaningful ways. Furthermore, waiting is intimately connected to the principle of witness in the journey of faith. As we wait for God's blessings on our endeavors, we are called to be living witnesses to His love and grace in the world. This means actively sharing our faith with others, serving those in need, and shining the light of Christ in every area of our lives. Our witness is not just about what we say; it's about how we live our lives and the example we set for others. As we work diligently and serve faithfully while waiting for God's blessings, we become living testimonies to His faithfulness and provision, inspiring others to trust in Him and His promises. Moreover, our waiting season provides us with unique opportunities to minister to those around us and make a positive impact on their lives. It's often during times of waiting that we have the most significant influence on others, as they observe our faithfulness and perseverance in the face of adversity. Our willingness to trust in God's timing and continue working diligently and serving faithfully despite the challenges we face can serve as a powerful testimony to those who are watching, drawing them closer to God and His kingdom. In conclusion, waiting, work, and witness are interconnected principles that play a vital role in the journey of faith. As we wait for God's blessings on our endeavors, we are called to continue working diligently and serving faithfully, trusting in His perfect timing and providence. Our waiting season provides us with an opportunity to grow and develop into the person God wants us to be, as we are refined and molded by His hand. And as we wait and work, we are called to be living witnesses to God's love and grace in the world, sharing our faith with others and shining the light of Christ in every area of our lives. By embracing these principles and actively engaging with God's plan for our lives, we can experience His blessings and fulfill His purposes for us in ways beyond our wildest imagination.

Five

Win

The concept of winning extends far beyond mere victory in a competition; it embodies a mindset—a way of approaching life with determination, optimism, and gratitude. In 1 Corinthians 9:24, the apostle Paul uses the analogy of a race to illustrate this mindset, reminding us that while all runners may compete, it's those who run with purpose and determination who ultimately claim the prize. Similarly, embracing a winning mindset is about running our own race with intentionality and perseverance, staying focused on our goals, maintaining a positive attitude, and recognizing the hard work that has brought us success. At the heart of a winning mindset is a clear sense of purpose—a driving force that propels us forward even in the face of obstacles and challenges. It's about knowing what we want to achieve and why it matters to us, and channeling our energy and efforts towards that goal with unwavering determination. Just as a runner focuses on the finish line, so too must we keep our eyes fixed on our objectives, refusing to be deterred by setbacks or distractions along the way. Moreover, running with purpose requires a deep understanding of our strengths, weaknesses, and values. It's about leveraging our unique talents and abilities to their fullest potential, while also acknowledging areas where we may need to grow or improve. By aligning our actions with our values and staying true to ourselves, we can navigate the challenges of life with integrity and authenticity, knowing that we are living in accordance with our deepest convictions. In the pursuit of our goals, maintaining a positive attitude is essential. It's about cultivating a mindset of optimism and resilience, even in the face of adversity. While obstacles and setbacks are inevitable, it's our response to them that ultimately determines our success. By choosing to see challenges as opportunities for growth and learning, we can overcome even the most daunting obstacles with grace and determination. Moreover, a positive attitude is contagious, inspiring those around us to believe in themselves and their abilities. Just as a runner's determination can motivate others to push themselves harder, so too can our optimism and resilience serve as a beacon of hope for those who may be struggling. By embodying positivity in all that we do, we can create a ripple effect of encouragement and empowerment that uplifts everyone involved. As we journey towards our goals, it's important to take time to recognize and celebrate our successes along the way. Whether big or small, each victory is a testament to our hard work, dedication, and perseverance. By acknowledging our achievements with gratitude and humility, we not only affirm our progress but also reinforce our commitment to continuous growth and improvement. Celebrating success is also an opportunity to express gratitude for the support and encouragement of those who have helped us along the way. Just as a runner relies on the cheers of the crowd to fuel their determination, so too do we draw strength from the encouragement of our friends, family, and mentors. By expressing gratitude for their contributions to our success, we not only honor their efforts but also strengthen the bonds of community and fellowship that sustain us on our journey. Finally, embracing a winning mindset requires us to stay humble and committed to continuous growth. It's about recognizing that success is not an endpoint but a journey—a journey marked by progress, setbacks, and opportunities for learning and development. By remaining humble in the face of success, we guard against complacency and remain open to new challenges and opportunities for growth. Moreover, staying committed to growth means embracing a mindset of lifelong learning and improvement. Just as a runner seeks to improve their time with each race, so too must we continually strive to become the best versions of ourselves. Whether through further education, skills development, or personal reflection, there are always opportunities to learn and grow, no matter where we are on our journey.

As we delve deeper into the integration of Wisdom, Work, Witness, and Wait with the concept of winning, we uncover a profound synergy that underpins our journey towards success and fulfillment. Each of these elements plays a crucial role in shaping our mindset, guiding our actions, and ultimately determining our outcomes. At the heart of it all lies wisdom—

the foundational principle that informs and empowers every aspect of our journey. Without wisdom, our efforts are futile, our actions aimless, and our dreams mere fantasies. It is through wisdom that we gain the guidance and strength we need to navigate the challenges of life and turn our dreams into reality. Wisdom serves as the cornerstone of our journey towards winning, providing us with the knowledge, discernment, and insight necessary to make informed decisions and seek divine guidance. It is through wisdom that we recognize the importance of aligning our goals and actions with God's will, acknowledging that true success comes not from our own understanding but from trusting in the wisdom of a higher power. Without wisdom, our efforts are driven by self-reliance and pride, leading us down paths of uncertainty and disappointment. It is only through seeking wisdom from God that we can find the clarity and direction we need to chart a course towards victory. Moreover, wisdom reminds us of our limitations as human beings and the need for divine guidance and strength in all that we do. Our human minds and bodies are too weak to achieve anything of lasting significance on our own. It is only through the strength and wisdom that comes from God that we can overcome obstacles, persevere through challenges, and achieve our goals. As Proverbs 3:5-6 reminds us, "Trust in the Lord with all your heart and lean not on your own understanding; in all your ways submit to him, and he will make your paths straight." By seeking wisdom from God and trusting in His guidance, we can navigate the complexities of life with confidence and assurance, knowing that He will direct our steps and lead us to victory. While wisdom provides us with the guidance and strength we need to navigate the journey towards winning, it is through work that we put that wisdom into action. Work serves as the path to progress, propelling us towards our goals through diligent effort and dedication. It is through our work that we demonstrate our faith and commitment to achieving success, knowing that our efforts are not in vain but are working towards a greater purpose. However, it's important to recognize that work alone is not enough to guarantee success. Without the guidance and strength that comes from God, our efforts are limited, and our achievements fleeting. It is only through combining our work with wisdom—seeking divine guidance and strength—that we can truly achieve lasting success. As James 1:5 reminds us, "If any of you lacks wisdom, you should ask God, who gives generously to all without finding fault, and it will be given to you." By combining our work with wisdom, we can navigate the challenges of life with grace and resilience, knowing that God is with us every step of the way. Moreover, having a winning mindset from the beginning can significantly enhance our ability to achieve success. A winning mindset is characterized by determination, optimism, and gratitude, and it serves as a powerful catalyst for turning our dreams into reality. By approaching life with a positive attitude and a belief in our ability to succeed, we can overcome obstacles, persevere through challenges, and achieve our goals with confidence and determination. However, it's important to recognize that having a winning mindset does not mean that we don't have to work hard. On the contrary, it is through our diligent effort and dedication that we demonstrate our commitment to achieving success and fulfilling our potential.

As we work towards our goals with wisdom and a winning mindset, we are called to be living witnesses to our faith through our words and actions. Witness is about sharing our journey with others, serving those in need, and spreading positivity and encouragement wherever we go. It is through our witness that we inspire others to believe in themselves and their abilities, and to trust in God's plan for their lives. Moreover, witness serves as a reminder of the importance of aligning our actions with our values and beliefs. Just as a faithful steward manages their resources in accordance with their master's wishes, so too must we steward our lives in a manner that reflects our commitment to following Christ. By serving others with love, compassion, and humility, we embody the teachings of Jesus and make His love tangible to those around us. Finally, as we journey towards winning with wisdom, work, and witness, we inevitably encounter the challenge of waiting. Waiting is not a passive state of being but an active engagement with God's timing and providence. It is through waiting that our faith is tested and refined, and our character molded into the image of Christ. However, it's important to recognize that waiting is not a sign of weakness but of trust and surrender to God's perfect timing. As we wait for God's blessings on our endeavors, we are called to remain steadfast in our faith, trusting in His promises even when they seem distant or unreachable. It is through waiting that we learn to surrender our desires and ambitions to God's will, knowing that His plan unfolds in His timing. By embracing the waiting season with hope and confidence, we can endure the challenges of life with grace and resilience, knowing that God is with us every step of the way. In conclusion, the integration of wisdom, work, witness, and wait with winning reveals a profound synergy that underpins our journey towards success and fulfillment. By seeking wisdom from God, putting our faith into action through diligent work, being living witnesses to His love and grace, and patiently waiting on His timing, we can navigate the complexities of life with confidence and assurance, knowing that He who promised is faithful to fulfill His word.

Conclusion

As we draw near to the conclusion of our journey through the five W's to success—Wisdom, Work, Witness, Wait, and Win—we are reminded of the timeless wisdom and guidance found in the pages of Scripture. From Genesis to Revelation, the Bible serves as a roadmap for navigating the complexities of life and finding true success and fulfillment in God's perfect plan. As we reflect on the principles and practices outlined in this book, let us anchor our hearts and minds in the promises of God, drawing strength and inspiration from His Word as we press forward on our journey towards victory. The importance of seeking divine wisdom is echoed throughout Scripture, with passages such as Proverbs 2:6 reminding us that "the Lord gives wisdom; from his mouth come knowledge and understanding." In the pursuit of success, let us never lean on our own understanding, but instead trust in the wisdom of God to guide our steps and direct our paths. By seeking His guidance through prayer, meditation on His Word, and reliance on the Holy Spirit, we can navigate the challenges of life with clarity and confidence, knowing that He will make our paths straight. Scripture is replete with exhortations to work diligently and wholeheartedly in everything we do. Colossians 3:23 reminds us to "work heartily, as for the Lord and not for men," recognizing that our efforts are ultimately unto the glory of God. As we strive towards our goals, let us commit ourselves to excellence in all things, knowing that our labor in the Lord is never in vain (1 Corinthians 15:58). Whether in our careers, relationships, or personal pursuits, may we approach each task with diligence and dedication, trusting in God to bless the work of our hands. As followers of Christ, we are called to be living witnesses to His love and grace in the world. Matthew 5:16 urges us to "let your light shine before others, so that they may see your good works and give glory to your Father who is in heaven." In the pursuit of success, let us never lose sight of our calling to be salt and light in a world in need of hope and healing. Whether through acts of kindness, words of encouragement, or sharing our faith with others, may we boldly proclaim the transformative power of the gospel and lead others into a deeper relationship with Christ. In the midst of our journey towards success, we are often called to wait patiently on the Lord, trusting in His perfect timing and providence. Psalm 27:14 reminds us to "wait for the Lord; be strong, and let your heart take courage; wait for the Lord!" As we encounter delays, setbacks, and obstacles along the way, let us anchor our hope in the promises of God, knowing that He is faithful to fulfill His word. Though the waiting season may be difficult, it is through patient endurance that our faith is strengthened and our character refined, preparing us for the blessings that lie ahead. Finally, as we reach the culmination of our journey, let us celebrate the victories that God has already won on our behalf. 1 Corinthians 15:57 reminds us that "thanks be to God, who gives us the victory through our Lord Jesus Christ!" In Christ, we have been given the ultimate victory over sin, death, and the powers of darkness, and nothing can separate us from the love of God (Romans 8:37-39). As we press forward on our journey towards success, let us do so with confidence and assurance, knowing that the God who has already conquered the grave is with us every step of the way.

To all who have journeyed with me through the pages of this book, I offer a word of encouragement and hope. Regardless of where you find yourself in your pursuit of success, know that you are not alone. God is with you, guiding your steps, strengthening your faith, and empowering you to overcome every obstacle that stands in your way. As you continue on your journey, may you find comfort and strength in the promises of God, knowing that He who began a good work in you will bring it to completion (Philippians 1:6). May you walk in wisdom, work with diligence, witness with boldness, wait with patience, and ultimately experience the joy of victory in Christ Jesus. In closing, I leave you with the words of Joshua 1:9: "Be strong and courageous. Do not be frightened, and do not be dismayed, for the Lord your God is with you wherever you go." May these words be a source of strength and encouragement to you as you continue on your journey towards success and fulfillment. May you walk in the wisdom of God, work with diligence and dedication, witness with boldness and compassion, wait with patience and trust, and ultimately experience the fullness of victory that comes from knowing and serving our Lord and Savior, Jesus Christ. Amen.